The Origins of the Easter Bunny

Ian Lightsey

Thirdlight
Publishing

The Origins of the Easter Bunny
Text and illustrations copyright © 2023 by Ian Lightsey

All rights reserved. No portion of this book may be reproduced in any form without written permission from the publisher or auther, except as permitted by U.S. copyright law. Any references to historical events, real people, or real places are used fictitiously. Names, characters, and places are products of the author's imagination.

First Edition

Published by Ian Lightsey
Typeset in Caroni
Visit the author's website at www.thirdlightpublishing.com

ISBN: 979-8-9884874-0-1 (paperback)
ISBN: 979-8-9884874-1-8 (ebook)
Library of Congress Control Number: 2023910583

For Cora

There once was a bunny in the early days –

in the grass she hopped,

For a man they called Jesus was judged on a cross, and died for the sins of all who are lost.

After the sun had fallen,
Jesus was carried away.

They took Him from Calvary to a cold, dark cave.

The bunny peered up the hill – the cave was so far away!

She thought, "What will He eat? How long will He stay?"

"I think I can make it, but it may take a few days."

"I don't have much – I'll give what I can…"

"Jesus deserves more than He was given by man."

So that bunny filled up her basket with carrots and eggs,

and climbed up that mountain with her short, little legs!

The sun rose and set and on the third day,

she was taken aback by what she saw in the cave...

Strips of linen without Jesus inside –

"How unexpected!" She thought, as she sighed.

As she passed by a house on her way back home,

she looked down at her basket as she knelt in the loam.

"Jesus may not need this, but someone else might –"

"I don't want to knock since it's the middle of the night!"

So that little bunny carefully placed
that basket she'd carried with so much grace,

softly down in front of the door,
just in case this family needed it more.

As she made her way down to her home on the hill, she couldn't help but notice the air wasn't so still -

Darting and flitting, the breeze danced through the trees –

tossing and twisting the branches with ease!

Her long ears floated like sails in the wind,
and her little pink nose twitched with every passing scent.

"Something feels different, but what, I can't say – I'm just a bunny at the end of the day!"

The sunset, the moon,

and the sky full of stars,
sang:

"Hosanna! Hosanna!"

to Jesus, the man with the scars...

From the Author:

Thank you for allowing me to share this story with your family! It's an honor to be part of your Easter celebration as we honor Him. I hope this tale blesses you and provides an avenue to share His love with others.

As a self-published author, I don't have the same influence over the printing process or quality as traditional publishers do. If the quality of your book's printing and/or binding is lacking in any way, please contact me at support@thirdlightpublishing.com and I will make every effort to rectify the situation.

I hope to bring additional titles to print in hardcover as well as board book formats as they become economically viable - thank you so much for your support!

Regards,

Ian Lightsey, Thirdlight Publishing

Made in the USA
Las Vegas, NV
02 April 2025